the flap pamphlet series

A Suburb of Heaven

open, read, turn

A Suburb of Heaven

the flap pamphlet series (No. 17)
Printed and Bound in the United Kingdom

Published by the flap series, 2017
the pamphlet series of flipped eye publishing
All Rights Reserved

Cover Design by Petraski
Series Design © flipped eye publishing, 2010
Author Photo © Pnina Shinebourne, 2017

ISBN-13: 978-1-905233-52-6

A Suburb of Heaven

Pnina Shinebourne

Contents | *A Suburb of Heaven*

I
A Suburb of Heaven

Poems reimagining the life and work of Stanley Spencer

Nails

splayed
between his teeth
nails tucked
behind his ears
nails piercing
the air –
under his cap
the workman
in orange vest
spreads
a grin-shaped lip.
Come on
his mate is saying
let's bang a nail
into the palm.

Someone adjusts
the crown of thorns
a boy fastens
the thief's arms
people gather
in the high street.
Behind net curtains
eyes sneak
at a woman lying
on a heap of rubble
arms outstretched

still as a stone.
And it is quiet −
a silence
drifting like dust.

And it was art
the workman said
I was proud to be
in his painting
I had to keep grinning
but my mouth was stuffed with nails.

Capture

the bodies in a grid of pencil lines
against a flower-spattered wallpaper.
Set the point between touching
and cringing, between your legs
stretching out towards her thighs
and her turned-off stare; between
your spectacled pair of eyes
longing to huddle in the folds
of her flesh and her frozen-faced
look, cutting you off
midway between her navel
and her breasts, sandwiched by
a burning stove and an uncooked
supper, a cold blood-red leg of meat.

Wrapped

in a billowing dressing gown and slippers, father
strides off in the high street, plump chicken in tow.
There was a clutter of angels in the backyard.

The shadows zigzagged on the roof.
Heaven was on the left. A parked car blocked the gate.
John Donne arrived through a side entrance.

Clouds

jostled across the sky, throwing
patches of dusk on the wallpaper.

You could climb up to the window,
watch the towpath skidding its way

to the river. In the garden below, Joseph
was doing something to a chestnut tree.

Mary was looking at the infant in his crib.
There was a jungle of brambles by the fence.

Inside a man wrapped chubby arms
around a woman. Their lips touched.

Shadows romped about the hedge, painting
a little darkness in the background.

Wild

geese fly over the camp where the clouds
touch the hills, watchmen rise
from trenches cut clean into the crust
of the earth;   above the river
a scrawny soldier in shirtsleeves
scrubs his underpants.

He remembers a lineup of shirts,
sleeves flapping in the morning
wind. Outside the iron gate
two boys play marbles
and a rag-and-bone man collects
empty beer bottles; a girl in white.
A tune, perhaps a sigh pours out
of her wide-open mouth;

and along the garden wall, slumped
against a step, a man stripped
to grey-white underwear, drifts off
in hazy sun. Perhaps
it is simple – a snooze
in the breeze – but for a tingle
in his face, half-way between
drunkenness and reverie,
between a villager and a saint.

Flickers of Michelangelo's
wingless angels flame at him
lighten up his mind,
uplifted for now but never
quite relieved from the cry
of wild geese, flying.

He

sees a hand rising from the sleeve
of her jumper as she pulls back the lid
of the boat-shaped grave and rolls
her shadow around the stone.
A tomb opens up like pages of a book
unfurling in a gust of wind.
Six prophets doze off along the church wall.

A memory pours its soul down his eyes –
Mr Francis the baker returns from doughing:
White all over. Swans trundle down the street
in a wheelbarrow.   Virginia creeper
falls like soft green icicles.
Unhappenings.
The prophets are stranded in a suburb of heaven.

Perched

on a stool, his back to the window,
an artist mixing paint on a palette
  – blue with a dash of yellow –
feels a distant tremor
through his fingers, an echo
of a splash: a child swimming
in a pathway of sunlight
sees a girl in a punt
emptying a teapot in the river.

It is summer. Boats slip adrift.
A figure in a straw hat sitting
in a wicker chair on a ferry,
an oar drips over his shoulder.
He leans forward, dazzled,
just up from keeling over.
It is Christ. Preaching
at the regatta. A boy stares,
mouth wide open.   On the bridge
cars sway in a breeze of prayers,
and along the bank a flock of girls
spy a couple lolling behind a hedge.

The artist adjusts his spectacles
I want them in a state of joy, he says,
someone lights a Chinese lantern,
people dance on the hotel lawn,
two disciples laze in their deckchairs

watching swans glide past;
the disciples are a bit bored,
he says, *they have heard it all before.*
On the riverbank Mr Brookes feeds his chicken.

Look

at the sea   ghost-like   dusky dark-blue horizon   all ribbed
a gleaming froth along each rib   shadows of ships
and hills beyond   all bronze.   Dismount at railhead
taken in ration oxcarts along track   oxen swaying
under yokes   heads stretched forward   heat pouring down
soldiers burn a firebreak around camp.
Sound of scrunching gravel   maybe a cart in the road.
                    Faint smoke
rising from beyond no-man's-land
                    the feeling of them nearby

A Second Life

She is nameless, a girl in a painting lying
on a brown-white striped bedspread,

dead (so it is told). Through a window,
beyond a potted geranium on the ledge,

you see a man stretching out his arm
to touch her, a dazzling glow in his eyes.

And around the bed, feet jostling
on the spotted rug, onlookers gasp, startled

as her body shudders, unfurls faintly
and dissolves into life.

His fingers flutter over her skin,
peeling death off her face.

But you see her looking back, weary,
eyelids drooping, a shadow crossing her face.

He brings her back to life (so it is told)
but he can't make her laugh, or love.

Sketch

I paint you in your wedding dress, fingers
splayed, showing off your lace-net gloves;
or flopped in your chair with cushions
pushing against the hollow of your back.
I could add an archangel sitting by your side;
instead I sketch myself in, spraying white
lilies over your body at dusk.

Flicking

up my pincers, I curl my tail in a striking
arch, my heart flutters in the desert heat.
A prickle flows through the slits of my legs,
sets free the hiss, the song of cuticles,
the spectacle of my sting.

This morning I sensed a quiver in the sand,
a stranger here, kneeling by a shadowless
shrub, reaching out to touch my claws.
Oh! the thrill of the squeeze.
But there was something about him, a softness
I liked when he held me in his palm –
my sting a prayer in his hand.

Captured

in a grid of pencil lines, lying naked
in crumpled sheets   her legs wide apart.
He is squatting between the burning
stove and the uncooked supper, midway
between her navel and her breasts,
feet pointing towards her thighs;
his bulgy eyes creep into dimples
of flesh, crawl over a crease between
a curve of her shoulder and raised
armpit, skim a cringe at her mouth's edge.
He posed her there but can't make her
touch his hairy chest, the saggy paunch,
nor turn her face towards him, or smile.
Her eyes trace a cold blood-red leg of meat.

When

cabbage was cooked in boiling water
it was like rotten eggs stinking.
When iron was sizzled in the blazing forge
it was like a bright-red tiger hissing.

When a comet hurled its tail in the sky
there were sparkles and thunder and bumping
like the world was tumbling down roaring.

When she knelt in the street, eyes shut,
praying for the world to hang on tight,
three angels came for an earthly visitation.

The former Old Forge is now a local Tandoori,
cabbage is cooked in fried onion or garlic;
the taste is nutty and crunchy
with a tinge of ginger and rosewater.

Amid

fleshy bulging bodies
scraggy chicken claw hands
stockings heels legs   feet
a jumble of flyblown lovers
in open-mouthed devotion,
amid misshapen yearnings
he perceived his subject –
the beloved of his imaginings

Sitting

there watching
cobwebs huddled
in the corner
he saw
toes stepping
on the floorboards
a woman
(once his wife)
slipping away
at the edge
of the window
and their daughter
holding tight
to a doll
with black holes
for eyes.

Socks

strewn on the floor – socks
picked up for twelve years
stiff with sweat   thinning at the heel

a glimpse of skin at the ball of his foot
where the weave was worn out,
his feet crossed at the ankles

toes pointing at opposite corners
sometimes touching her foot
sometimes not.

Among

strewn cabbage leaves, bread-crusts too
hard to chew, a double edged comb of fish
bone and crumpled paper in overflowing dustbins;

amid empty beer bottles and a thicket of rust-
mottled pipes, he found his subject
at the edge of a brushstroke –   a glimpse

of heaven in the shape of a cabbage leaf
and a shimmering dot of sunlight
crawling over a teapot cracked at the spout.

II
Anna O.

Poems reimagining the case history of Anna O. (the patient who 'invented' psychoanalysis)

This girl, who was bubbling over with intellectual vitality, led an extremely monotonous existence in her puritanically- minded family. She embellished her life in a manner which probably influenced her decisively in the direction of her illness, by indulging in systematic day-dreaming, which she described as her 'private theatre' (Freud & Breuer, Studies on Hysteria).

Pas de Deux

Transference, said Freud, the deep shape
of everything; *folie a deux,*
folie furieuse, or *pas de deux*
of the sugar plum fairy and her cavalier
on first night bash –
bodies arching to each other's grasp,
tangled in the web of the dance

A Slice of Dream

In a woman troubled by hysterika, or having a difficult labour,
a sneeze is a good thing   (Hippocrates, aphorism 5.35)

Hysteria is a scream. In those far-off days
wanderlustful wombs freefloated
between the hammocked wetlands,
prolapsed downwards,
or clambered on into the swelter
upward to the thorax –
in a word, altogether erratic.
Sometimes a woman's mouth splayed
in a scream, strained to sneeze
the errant womb back into place.
When it remains barren too long
after puberty, said Plato,
it is distressed and sorely disturbed,
straying in the body.

                    *

The year the Donau froze over
ice-wind hugged an early evening
unfurling the lace curtains.
In the darkened room Doctor Breuer
massaged Fräulein Anna's leg,
his hand running the seam of her stocking.
Hysteria, he said. She sneezed.
The element of sexuality was astonishingly
undeveloped in her, the doctor noted
as the evening plunged.
A snake slithered along her arm
working its way in a quiver.

Snakeheads raced around the room. Words
tumbled
   splintered into shreds
                 ja m a i s
        no – body
  bella mia
          p l
              e a se
                   liebchen
       Nu i t.

         *

The fire breast stared at them, smouldering
its mouth. Puffs of smoky bits
sailed back and forth between their eyes.
Chimney sweeping, said Fräulein Anna,
thrusting a slice of dream towards him,
chewy and crumbly.
It's the talking cure, my private theatre,
she said, dimming the stage lights.

Notes for an Autobiography

1

[Eight years old, captivated by the biblical story of Joseph]

(Not) Learning the Bible with father

What does it mean שִׁכְבָה עִמִּי? I ask.
Papa and I are reading the Bible.
He tries to skip to the next chapter,

too late, I insist.   Lie by me, he says,
like when you sleep in Mama's
and Papa's bed after a bad dream.
Was he naked? I ask.
Liebchen, father says, let's read
the *Froschkönig* instead.

2

[Fifteen years old, still fascinated by the story of Joseph, hiding 'naughty' prints in her wardrobe]

(Not) Learning Art History at the Catholic Girls' School

A woman's body twisted in crumpled sheets,
halfway towards him, half turned away.
The angle isn't flattering: shaggy hair,
dimples bobbing about on a bare thigh,
dress slipped off her shoulders.
His head pulls to *Exit* but his eyes
look back; his hand stretched to grab

34

her breast – or is he pushing her away?
I see her tugging at his pants, clutching
something   trapped   stiffening

עָמִי שֶׁכְבָה (Hebrew) – pronounced *shichvá eemméé*
Froschkönig (German) – Frog Prince
The print is Rembrandt's etching, *Joseph and Potiphar's Wife*

Twinge

After Kei Miller

It was nothing really –
just a twinge of heart
something she hadn't dreamt
all the way through
her world was neither here
    nor there
            with father
neither   here nor there
        with herself.
    A world
        which did not know
 if it would stay
                or go.

Notes for a Case History

That night, sitting by her father's bedside, in a waking dream she saw a black snake slithering towards the patient. She felt her fingers turning into little snakes with death's heads fingernails.

Alone with a little deformed man with long nails squatting on the floor gibbering.

She tried to keep the snake off, but her right arm was paralysed, cut off.

Cut off, unable to communicate. She could not raise her finger any more, trapped in bricks meeting her wherever she turned.

Unable to utter a sound, she could find no   tongue in which to speak.

Estranged from words, curled up beyond the edge of speech.

Profound darkness in her head, the terror of not being able to think, of becoming blind and deaf.

A deep pool of sticky water closed over her head. She saw nothing and heard nothing.

Patient

In this darkened room she could be
any patient, the slumped figure
you see in the dim lamplight
head propped up on a soft pillow
arm drooping by her bedside
                                        lifeless.

Yet her right fist is clenched
and who knows what wells up
under the drapes of her silk
dressing gown throbbing
to unfurl.   Remember the times
she felt your hands, skin rippling
in the dark?   How you'd massage
her legs once in a while?
How she held your gaze? You both
wanting it to last.
                                        You can't

explain the stirrings you felt,
how you got drawn to the lure
of her spell or where you imagined
this would leave her
                    but lost

Love Bites

After Rosemary Tonks

My spirit broke her fast on you,
lapped the tender radiance
of your gaze, gulped down the balmy
words, the morsels of your charm.
You fed her with a stroke of hand,
peeled off the crossed-out bits;
your voice caressed my ears
beyond a horizon lost in mist
until memory burst its hinge.
And you took it all, unwrapped its folds,
replayed the pieces of my life,
reshaped, retold, blown away,
all but the love-bite of your touch.
And, very softly, I damn you for it.

Delirium

How we have waited! Words paced the air
      stumbled over   kicked back
     surged through the conference hall.

I stood by the slide in a chain of signifiers
making holes in meanings.
Tongue tangled syllables swept the floor
sprinted back and forth   gliding
       down the aisles.

Misadventure of desire at the hedges
of jouissance, said the analyst.
Ein wissenshaftliches Märchen, said the sexologist,
  and blew
a trail of smoke into my face.

A memory falling like tender snowflakes
down my eyes –
     father trickling over the page
a face uploading a bustle
painted a little sadness in the background.
See the shadows romping about the hedge,
said the professor, possible significance
of childhood object loss …
Just the opposite! Cried a delegate,
sexuality is the dynamo of the gas-tap,
a peacock's feather tickling the belly

of a pretty woman ...
    unnavigable river ... Exactly!
Here, quick! A chimney sweeper
climbed into the sooty delirium
                                trilled
    the Falsetto, flipping his tongue
in bel canto sensibility.

I caught a glimpse of interpretation
peeling off the crust between the psyche
and the drowned pain – an echo
of a splash in cold water. On the bridge
cars swayed in a breeze of prayers.

Blue Angel

After Anne Carson

It is also true I dream about snakeheads
racing around the room
and have done so
since the day I read
in the published volume of Freud/Jung letters
(this was years after I left Vienna)
a sentence which I shall quote in full.
Freud's letter to Jung 21.11.1909:
Chimney sweeping is an action symbolic
of coitus, something Breuer never dreamed of.
     Freud hesitates to name me
        but
let me tell you
there was no
     cold sweat.
     Here
I could translate Lacan
(Breuer bit the bait that Anna O. offered him
but Freud was neurotic) or show you
the Blue Angel
close up:
face spills into the mirror
mouth curves
     smoke curls down the chimney
fingers fumble   flustered
spun in spiderwebs

giddy
         unwinged.
      Smell of burnt cigar.
.   I remember him every time someone is blowing smoke.

Stamp

When he was not   playing chess   in the evening
my father   would sometimes   clear the dinner table
immerse   torn bits   of old envelopes   in a bowl
of lukewarm water   to let   the glue dissolve
and peel   the stamps off the paper.   Touching
the stamps   with your fingers was strictly forbidden.
Like butterfly wings he said   you can rub off their
scales with your fingers. That was   when I saw her
floating   on the surface   face up   a blue-grey-
long-nosed profile serene intense.   There was
something written in a language I didn't understand
helper of humanity father said   carefully   checking
the stamp   with a magnifying glass.   When she was
young   her nickname was Anna   Anna O   he said.

Anna O.'s real name was Bertha Pappenheim. Following a long convalescence she became a pioneering social worker and writer, campaigning for women's rights and against prostitution and trafficking in women. In 1954 West Germany honoured her with a special postage stamp in recognition of her work. The stamp was one of a series dedicated to 'Helpers of Humanity'.

Acknowledgements

I am grateful to Jo Shapcott and Mimi Khalvati for their continuing support and critical engagement with my work.

Some of the poems (or earlier versions of) appeared in Iota and Ariadne's Thread. Four poems from the *A Suburb of Heaven* sequence appear in *Stanley Spencer Poems An Anthology* (Two Rivers Press)

A Suburb of Heaven is indebted to the following sources:

Bell, Keith (1992) *Stanley Spencer: a Complete Catalogue of the Paintings,* London: Phaidon Press.

Glew, Adrian (2001) *Stanley Spencer: Letters and Writings,* London: Tate Publishing.

Pople, Ken (1996) *Stanley Spencer,* London: Harper Collins.

Inverclyde Shipbuilding Reminiscences: https://sites.google.com/site/inverclydeshipbuilding/home/reminiscences

Anna O. is indebted to the following sources:

Borch-Jacobsen, M. (1996). *Remembering Anna O.: A Century of Mystification.* New York: Routledge.

Forrester, J. (1986). *The true story of Anna O. In The Seductions of Psychoanalysis: Freud, Lacan and Derrida.* Cambridge: Cambridge University Press.

Freud, S., & Breuer, J. (1895). *Studies on Hysteria. Vol. 2.* London: Hogarth Press.

Guttmann, M. G., & Pappenheim, B. (2001). *The enigma of Anna O.: A biography of Bertha Pappenheim.* Moyer Bell Limited.

Lightning Source UK Ltd.
Milton Keynes UK
UKHW010721210321
380690UK00002B/96

9 781905 233526